AF327181

ROBIN HOOD IN THE DARK AGES

KELVIN CORCORAN

ROBIN HOOD IN THE DARK AGES

Preface by Tom Raworth

Permanent Press
London & New York
1985

Cover Design by Ray Seaford

The cover drawing, "Wound Man", depicting injuries suffered by combatants, is from the works of the 16th-century surgeon Ambroise Paré, and is reproduced in Owen H. Wangensteen and Sarah D. Wangensteen's *The Rise of Surgery*.

Grateful acknowledgement is made to the following magazines, in which many of these poems first appeared: *Figs, Global Tapestry, Molly Bloom, Ninth Decade, Reality Studios,* and *Rock Drill* in the United Kingdom, and *Island* in Canada.

British Library Cataloguing in Publication Data

Corcoran, Kelvin
    Robin Hood in the dark ages.
    I. Title
    821'.914   PR6053.066/

ISBN 0-905258-08-8

PREFACE

Twisting echoes form a trellis thought almost
loops around. Tone becomes stress; sense-changes,
metre. Imagination sees memory in a mirror and
swaps jokes. Light travels nerves to fire
emotions and self observes, notes down, makes
a clearing and has lunch.

> "if it's language
> there is the sun attendant warmth
> rising to meet it"

Kelvin Corcoran's first book of poems really
needs no introduction. *Robin Hood in the Dark
Ages* indeed. As I read, in Nottingham Town
a crowd gathers to worship ice-skaters and to
touch their Range Rover: in the Shire the
Sheriff's men arrest pickets.

> "The facts are known and they don't
> count. Where there is no vision the
> people perish."

      ... and a call for
vision is not a call to dream. I look forward
to his next book.

Tom Raworth
April, 1984

The Descartes Poems

DEEDS

the many facets of it, the radio
like bowls of light of thickening
walls what they say neighbours
in orbit about the heart a human
world as obvious as phenomenology as
the mind becomes actual here in
the European winter I have lit
the fire we have a mineral history to burn
and' we can't keep our hands off each other

your face that night through the windscreen
warming up, no satisfactory explanation I
have my wife my friend it is a Brandenburg
number one day occasions the gold breakfast
blue quilt, a Mexican girl talks at length
seagulls in a square garden lean into each
other on the surface horn's intaglio of happiness
sparkles the big gem of 24 hours

*

like the smell of nail varnish
comes in its gloss of sex occasion
to occasion a blanket lava
at the hearth, the things you do
in a plural sleep the absolute
message of perfect action each
word goes home in the deep gloss
of courage sun up open eyes
like a Germano Facetti the action
spills over the colours an extra
hard top-coat for the opening
core of Monday morning, you get there

JOHN LYNCH

going through these days
like Jean Dubuffet's busy life
wartime light enquiring buildings
pile white the sphinx on the needle,
clock face, a new suede jacket
handsome off the river marble air
blue distances build power houses of
common want, I'm light here January
shiny badge both ways the river
flowing too O flowers table a statement
if the heart greets even the river lights

GOING TO TOWN

1

could say heartline there
the palm's geometry of
impact speed ablaze with
a former collision does not happen here,
a contusion sinister to the line
if you see it it's all right
despite the red speed heartline
the passage of co-ordination
that your face is beauty so welcome
thank you   a perfect fit

2

the first lights of town, the fixed stars
on the fovea shine the arc of arrival
the neighbourhood dislocation shock absorbed
each day; go forward, kouroi diastole a charge
in the blood lights to both sides
and I'll be over by eight

3

a compositional device and the place
is all around you, unlike the market
up or down, the financial world tonight
but no change, the ports stay closed

along this retrospective silver laid
in the backward dark the line of attention
is relieved in the home light
you splash into town, a door closes opens

4

in town the roads and buildings
hang in safer speeds the duration
of civic use cushions children by the way
play ahead, slow take care here
daylight corridors the heat
from the shops spills onto
the street of people and the structured
light of leaves arranges a mutual speed,
drift ease the corner lean
into each other lives meet here

DESCARTES

1

Descartes came into the poem. He did not like his new job;
the way the chairs, the hi-fi and the fire lean into each other.
He came in, I have just cycled from Stockholm, there is a lot
of road between there and here. Times Square had soured
him, peeled off a few skins and measured the depth of green.
It is as I thought, the valve worked loose outside Paris.

It's not as if he is Malherbe either, across the field the slant
of December. Descartes couldn't give a toss for rounded
edges like playing cards, a Roman resting place; a holloway,
two on the way to work, the combined action of human and
natural agents—like I said, he didn't notice these details. He
changed my life, hat polish for a start and envy in the dark.

When he was tired, his mind elsewhere, tossing coconuts
at the poet's lawn, anywhere but here, Descartes would sit
and doze and fill the house with it. Brown, hairy, large. A
fistful of encased piss milk, remember no memory, the mind
elsewhere. The violated child, courage turn us now next the
light through the leaves, this path can be traced to the
Wiltshire border.

No, he would not take a walk but that dip down to the
brook is the boundary of the two villages. Yes, you can go
there, that's mine down to the brook. The horses of this
complex geometry are curious as you go.

2

Is it raining at my back or silence
high in the end of day head Monday
waits on shiny hill the conceptual sun
rises on the circuit of new green spring

a quick look at the Dantean stars
window open, foxes yap if the moon is full
no animal sleeps silver bangs through
the heart the field fills with light

a short time now, the unseparate events
come together, Linda's paintings dry
in the last heat blue roots against a fire,
other plants an unfixed surface of blue
light   these are the forces of victory

3

the money is on the table
on the way out I was zipped up
dark and tight, I was Frank
O'Hara's orphan brother
planning a windy route
through the new green spring of air

the money is road signs, turn the hard U
in love is Shakespeare's cum sweet luv
I would kiss your mouth and the secret
deep in its flesh of everything said
or will you he said well I'm glad
you're pleased by something, walking
out of a C19 novel and upstairs at speed

NO DEATH

combing out your blonde
using my cold hands I read
much of the weekend, draw out
£35 a week and try on that
soft crash on the bike
flop into the snow, I turned
to the traffic arms in air laughing
a hearse passes, the private joke
beats big death and always will

*

the watch stuck in table
varnish tingles the base
of the spine, love under
cover is how it begins
awake in the morning
and meet the white day breathing

*

de Kooning's face the chalk of March
on your tongue braille bird song, exciting
isn't it, he looked over the woman and
the room filled with light floats I thought
no that's not it   where then 3 o'clock and
it's spring, a face like the sun in another room

*

You can tell it's dry the lawn's
cracking, we've got a wet axe here
a loose blade, lambswool hurts no one
he was behaving like that
the wood swelling into the head
an abstract movement, if it's language
that is the sun attendant warmth
          rising to meet it

What Do You Mean
How Do You Find It

ROBIN HOOD

the hot symbolism of dawn rolls out
green and lush the air falls
over my head and onto my hands
the world pops up a 3D book

figures without obvious support,
there goes Robin Hood green like
the dawn the jolly mind
cross hatched with windows silver
trees and cars of the opposite row
sent spinning as day to day

there are different rooms where virtue
in a coat the colour of day
thats a nice coat, trust him
always the birds in the air
touch your face   the summer sky
fits like your favourite shirt

*

driving through the dread night of shire politics
rolling the sea swell and lunatic police cars
we have you John in our ears. Gloria, fruit
and carnival, carnival and sudden death

intention nouns its pleonastic way
"they must learn the principle of law and order"
her blonde pressure greens in the memory,
kiss me not her, one in the box the other raving
ah fuck it Frank, run from the madding crowd

Bach arranges the body about the instant of knowing
take a gun for example, an Italian apple
and the ocean of your cool hand
I held
            and would recommend to anyone

DOMESTIC AND FOREIGN POLICY

at this level crustacea stick to the hull
flourish and tatoo the hills
in soft whisky light like language
the crane flies bang themselves up on the light bulbs

the walls are built around a story of morning
in it a king is everyone rises for the work
in my pocket "Birds, Cattle, Fish & Flies"
at lunchtime too I go about
and watch the kids play football
slangy and blown up and down the sloping pitch

don't worry about turkey sandwiches
or previous talk, that was night
you touch all these things; a carpet of grass,
a silver currency and hand on shoulder
this tesserae of day flakes off and on
a 24 hour smile, the heart keeps it warm
then there is this line   really said
"send in the helicopters and morphine"

think hard but the days zero weekend
he is the red fruit of South Africa and the best of Costa Rica,
I think these South American governments
are fucking with my coffee,
I am a counter too, she leans over
hair up and back   the story breaks
holes in the day   darkness that doesn't

CARNIVAL

wanting a really better life we go to town
but the black wind of adulterous fucking birds us,
wash well baby, the trap door opens
the sea runs a corridor of sound through
the mind behind the sea wall
those cheap chalets where the old die,
another runs off where the flats fall back
to reveal ropes pulled by the three mayors
of newspaper repute and small town fecundities

set back from the weekend fields
the new medical centre in English light
takes off like a political campaign,
one arrow indicates forgotten exchanges
another, as big as the dark room says;
you will not leave this room again,
the lines of the exchange tied in one fat word
the unbelievable everything everyone wants to say,
fries the wires green and yellow

we gather the familiar corners and wide pavements
of human design where the talk fits
as sunlight moves across the fields of summer,
a generosity of children stand before their parents
the carnival comes, local schools and brass bands
parade flour and money in the air shining
has a clean sexual click for the vikings
     and girls with good legs

FOR JOHN LYNCH

I think city lawn lit in blocks
of night. Utopian but take care
in a poem with no story no
easy shine surface, other lives the radio
the crumpled paper and a taste of onions
that was a thing, she wept bitter
how many He takes, relieve my languish
a waterfall sounds in that line

No feeling, do not panic, wait
wait upstairs in bed I'll come soon
to weekend carpets flecked with doubt
and footprints to monday, tuesday
now sit   furniture not there gaps
they're better, friends not here
across half the country we went
foreign stations we picked up
old jazz in modern radio very sharp
wanting friends and one in loss
hold on   you can   each day to it

THE SEA THE FISH AND FISHERMEN

the whiting on the newspaper, markets crash
cars crash, he dangled three fish on three lines
silver dashes in the sunny day
a gold front is approaching the east coast.
I drive and talk from a tower of vanished guilt
bang   you hit the deck smoke rises from the roses
from the earth   print your hand on my face
says welcome down a corridor of sea and seagulls
unrolls a huge sky the human colour
pocketed by the better pool player
when you do dance, I wish you a wave of the sea

*

ancient kingdoms of you know
I am thinking of you face to face
a message nouns its pleonastic way

majascule I stand like an H and
release to the wind two sheets of the Daily Telegraph,
one returns straight into my hands
repeat   success   walk away across the lawn

I know I want you happy
in the middle of this
there's a dream or Linda Linda Linda,
in all of this is the world service
calling   Linda Linda Linda

A POLITICAL POEM

once John Wayne said, I'm just chilling this
the champagne in the ice bucket
in his hands like a prick
but that's fiction, the guns aren't real.

get inside your tiredness
step out of another skin-like
town of reversed light and public lies,
a safety net Platonic and pissy
see my chair just melted
I'm speaking from the floor
"No I wouldn't call these cuts excessive"

see that smoke, those clouds, they spell trouble
spelt Crazy Horse
who dreamt himself into the real world and fought
and hardest of all is to think and then act.
I tell you what we're going to do
      each thought has your face
      on its face   like a personal arrow
we're going to break into that vault
honeymoon in Paris and fuck the weather

*

I found a naked
jack, John I said, who
was dressed, I have
found this naked
jack discarded in the
grass we walk on
as conversation or
stick it in a poem
like this fleshy
beribboned jack
steam rises from the
teapot, steam rises from
the world springs
in our wake, seeds
in our socks

*

in town I wear a huge cowboy hat,
my mother laughs behind me
the wind in our faces

seven births five children
and poverty, she arrives
at love, my hat flaps its wings
my wife and my mother hold on
laughing as we go home

VOLITIONIST ECONOMICS

you're so dumb you don't even see
the treasure you're trampling with your own feet,
the motherload drained into every pocket,
my mother comes home in a liberty ship
baby by baby she brings heaven into the world.

all this happens in a particular light
for the farmer and his daughters,
the fruit ripe, the cows milk and
the spring rain focuses yes above the hill
in a green dress they cannot help but meet,
se habla Español?   you want   yes?
her celebrated girdle of bananas packed the house,
she became famous overnight

this is volitionist economics
the veins of gold glue the politics together,
lights go on in different rooms
architectonic agents plot and unplot,
you better talk fast they want answers
is this Rimini? Paterson? Gloucester? Lambeth?
I don't believe it but love it

THE RISE OF SURGERY

a picture of the wound man depicts
injuries suffered by combatants
and a map of the lighted areas of the globe
the spurious coasts and interiors of the white world.
a slit of daylight descends like glass
at the speed, at the speech of light
values zeroed in on him
a boy and girl, together with no past
lets...
thickened the blood and thinned the soldiers,
his jacket sort of Chinese but even looser

> what do you mean, how do you find it
> a basket of fruit in January
> a wasp on the coal, quite perky
> a new acquisition by Max Ernst

intention gets hit, the gone words scored on the heart
tramlines of hurt cross the sky touches the hill
clouds boom off into shops and darkness,
shopkeepers ride giant sex organs of corporate purpose
which is sport for all
or brutal toryism or
love me or leave me but don't leave me lonely.

he put his arm around the woman
but the ship is a tramp loaded with tractors,
chemicals and ten tons of Phos B 470/H.
don't be wet I am your father,
there is a fault   lights flicker the sea empties.
the captain came to calm them,
they saw the life jacket under his jumper.
Look at it this way, we're a microcosm of Hungarian society circa 16:
                 bailing out shit and illegal currency.

at night they bow their heads
the stars alight
and he dreams of Navaho wolfmen
the moon through the frosted pines of Dakota,
the blood is lovely dark and deep
sharp teeth like money, the fifth night of fog
in the grip of the weed
                        we will not abandon neonate fun
                        against the cliffs of night
                                a sort of rescue
                                a sort of jackpot

World Politics

WORLD POLITICS OR THE DIGESTIVE TRACT

in the living room of his voice
"no more dying" the martins have gone high
in sky dark august the lawn is grass covered,
cat opens mouth and green eyes
a literal song on the radio
that's a funny song, never grow old
cenotaph rocketed into space
England is free, soldiers don't
there are clouds of our boys
precipitate the distant ocean,
the African veldt has brutish men
but heroic animals tune in a major contentment,
like this cat stares and shiny
all over cat-look, radio I was thinking
soldiers don't, they just do

I make a little space, red wine expands
in a glass the wall below chrysanthemums
in jam jar water pink and pinker,
waiting for food opens doors
enzymes and things I can't imagine
my internal blue tubes
crimp the foody air

here comes the woman in a green jumper
a woman's life in her body walks about
my heart in orbit, O cat what she does for us
woman, cat and food my god
what a constellation, how fast it is
Linda when you're drunk
a superabundance of the green age
love I mean you, yes in your mouth

*

delay the speed of heroic film
and words go everywhere like cups of tea,
novels, pets and coins of an earthly issue
give I back I, that absence of politics
in a decent person the veins of gold
varicose the slack containment,
everything we don't do here

in magnetic august feel the rush
he sings, "fall into your human hands"
a woman walks by the cinema and
the dashboard lights up like a city,
a charm in this idle landscape like
an industry by Sheeler minus the machines,
the afternoons click over.
Stupid, you've lost all your money

this is a nice poem, a nice sausage, a nice man
but wait for the uncooked underbelly,
this is a cup of tea you can eat
better that the carpet appropriate
the peopled street, a plume of just look at us
majascule and not for sale,
like a charm to charm this idle country
run by shits for Shit & Shit in shit

I speak in my nice voice
so that's how you drive a car
use a phone, wear a shirt
we're all in this up to our eyes
Amor vincit omnia, I put my shoulder to Fortuna
I put my hand to drift in your hair,
casualty reports coming in
                              your hair is cool
                              human hand
                              hear that voice

THE LOST WORLD

there is a lost world, the table
I touch sunlights my hand
—do you want to go for a ride—
a film blue set-square to look through
sparrows on the lawn
and children in bikinis
my heart in its place
in the calendar of light

in English literature, said Churchill,
there are heroisms all round us
attended by Zambo our faithful servant
stuck up a beech tree like a white prick,
damn me, look at these apes
this is Babylon a Disney
"They must learn the principle of law and order"

sparrows and children in bikinis
ride hello in my heart
the calendar of light,
imagine a secret in yourself
of tv screen, carpet and chained hero
called first baby, it has a perfect face
and the powers in its hands push push push

A WOMAN A WOMAN

by the fact of a woman the baby floats
coral bones of the sea surround the house
called monday to monday, you do this
and that in its silvery light dots
encode a broadcast of perfect action
called a life together, called
monday to monday down the big dipper
going up in the clothes you wear
your nice trousers and airtex shirt,
there are flowers in the jar, pictures on the wall
and I'll clean the kitchen
cells hold it together, no arrows, no
a woman a woman

HOW IT CHANGES

funny how it changes everything
when the weather changes cloud the wind
in literal autumn, though it could be spring
the kitchen is different I am five days a week
the fridge hums your blonde hair
dressed in brown, we could do anything

this morning air balloons champion the sky,
address each other through a range of feelings
smile that smile, your money or your money,
like a big cast in an untethered domestic life
it's difficult to know what to wear
cold or hot, there are signs in the sky
like Habitat, Mothercare and Lux

all sorts place at ease an index,
I go home and shoot the furry apple
the hair grips and the cat shit,
the stations of the dial constellate your heart
his voice speaks, don't be flippant

A SLOGAN WILL NOT SUFFICE

the work of the sun, not illusion
diamonds hidden in the kitchen calendar
we pin them in the cork and shiny frame
bills and visits and mathematical stars,
like a deck of marked cards.
you are already here,
the trial of love that should be love
each word against each word
                            down of your arm
I look, lift in my heart

trust the occasional radar through the dark,
the cold wheel cash holds together
it is a plot against the chickens of America
the wealth rolls off the Atlantic in neat symbols;
one dark raindrop, a semicircle of sunrays,
a pigeon wings it on hard blue March,
your money or your money and then
Spring comes with obscene practices in the sky
                            from every part of the ranch
the boys came to meet the new boss,
the man of style   I float my legs
in the bath of this weather.
She saws through the bread down to the table
slices each period of life is conducted
in the way life is conducted
and stores the table in the polar box for summer.
Eat strawberries and run away,
the lungs open the shoulder blades spread
and it smells like bread, like petals and horse shit
in the massed scents of May.

In the spring of cash R.A.F. boys probe the hills,
farmers in tractors bravely waving, our boys in dungarees.
I walk in their film, you are in it, part of it.

Well captain, you look bitter, hurt and drunk.
I do?   Yes.   Well I am, just rub that for me and forget.
the trees scratch the fat sun
bad debts from the people we won't pay,
the postman said, silence in court the cat is pissing.

When I hear what it is meant to do to me
I hate it. I'd rather the flopped hollyhock
and yogurt lid, I'd rather the adverts
there is always music for your feelings, you are part of it,
like landscape in Thomas Hardy
under the heat of this traffic, beside yourself,
a man will leave if you fail, hello sir, it's me, Nic
on a horse taller than the hedge
he found a dead town formerly a zero
buzzed across the helloing girl
dark a girl garden decked in trees
families and traffic fresh from the word

this is not Wittgenstein or a dream you could dream in sleep,
below the arrow of the town map outside the library,
You are here. The roads travel from the varnished frame
around pink blocks on bleached green
the whole thing looks nasty and fucked up;
the police station, the play-with-me-houses
and the insanitary schools.
I think of their real colour
the same sun greens the real town
I think of how we could have lived
I think five aces, hit the deck or die

IMPUGN

I've done the crossword already,
ploughed shit into the hill all afternoon
calculate that gain, the sound of
E.E.C. grain climbs every mountain
I look at the pictures, unread the books
it's a gun battle outside the pueblo,
frozen smoke and no report

I've got the teapot ready
like a rocket for blast off
only need Linda now, to attack verbally?
bite?   not enough lettuce,
poets speak the air of plenty
litter airy words in the aesthete agents

(enough)

he drove a blue estate
he carried a shotgun
he robbed an off-license of £94,
on a Tuesday night, not much business
it was on the V.H.F. we were
in bed with a big moon

this is also a stupid crime

A statement

The streets crack and the hospitals smell. We are not the poor, we do not sweat under the ghost of a foreign policy. The furniture is carved out of sugar and white bread. Our fatty hearts are not cast in nylon, flog us more junk and we'll get better. Our women aren't uppity. He was a lovely baby but look at him now...this is impossible, nobody really says this—certainly not in a poem. She must be bemused at the stupidity that she has authorized. This is not the book of those fears, this is a message; the poor do not exist, you do not have to bother with them nor the children of the poor, sexualised at 10, 11 and 12. The facts are known and they don't count. Where there is no vision the people perish.

500 copies of this first edition, of which 50 are specially bound in heavy wrappers and are numbered and signed by the author, were published in 1985 as Number Thirteen in the Permanent Press series by Robert Vas Dias, 52 Cascade Avenue, London, N.10, England, and 1040 Park Avenue, New York, N.Y. 10028, U.S.A.